GW00655885

Maldon and Heybridge

in old picture postcards

by
Peter Came

European Library – Zaltbommel/Netherlands

Third edition: 1991

GB   ISBN 90 288 3224 6 / CIP

© 1985 European Library – Zaltbommel/Netherlands

INTRODUCTION

Maldon and Heybridge are two adjacent settlements, connected by an ancient causeway, on the Blackwater Estuary in Essex. Both gained historically from their respective importance as lowest bridge points on the River Chelmer and the River Blackwater. Heybridge is much older than Maldon with pre-Roman and Roman sites.

Maldon, meaning the hill marked by a cross, has been since Saxon times the more important of the two settlements. Its steep hill formed a defensive site for a burgh built in 916 by Edward the Elder, whose troops resisted the Danes in 917. Even later, the Danes were raiding this area and in 991 they sailed up the Estuary for Maldon. In the battle that ensued, immortalised in the Saxon poem, The Battle of Maldon, Brihtnoth, Ealdorman of Essex, was slain.

Heybridge was also a Saxon settlement, called Tidwoldington, but took the name of Heybridge c1200 when a high-arched bridge was built across the River Blackwater. Maldon and Heybridge, although so close, developed as two distinctly different settlements, but there was always rivalry and interaction between them. For one thing, until 1934 Maldon had been politically separate from Heybridge. In the Domesday Book, Maldon was the second most important town in Essex and since 1171 had enjoyed many privileges incorporated by Royal Charter, privileges that did not extend to Heybridge.

Maldon did not enjoy continuous prosperity and there is evidence that the fortunes of the Borough declined from the mid-sixteenth to the late eighteenth century. Its rival was always ready to take advantage. In 1618 coal was being imported into Heybridge without payment of dues to Maldon, with the result that *The Poor Porters attending to merchandise at The Heith and other tradesmen and Innkeepers have lost much...*

In character and political organisation, Maldon was always more urban, whereas Heybridge remained essentially a village until well after the opening of the Chelmer and Blackwater Navigation in 1797. In population, too, Maldon was always the larger settlement. In 1801 its population was 2,360 and by 1841 it had reached 3,967.

Heybridge was much smaller, but its growth was faster. In 1801, its population was 368; but in 1841 it had reached 1,177. Once the Navigation had opened, Heybridge industrialised rapidly with sites being occupied by Bentall's Works (1816) and by Maldon merchants who had moved to Heybridge. Maldon now had an industrial rival. The new docking facilities at Heybridge Basin enabled Heybridge to capture much of Maldon's mercantile trade. This is clearly shown in the increasing amounts of coal alone reaching Heybridge Basin compared with Maldon Hythe. In 1810 the figures respectively* were 26,711 and 12,380 tons. Heybridge's prosperity enabled some entrepreneurs to enter into Maldon's politics. Edward H. Bentall became Maldon's Liberal MP from 1868 to 1874.

The depression of the 1880s and railway competition were to have their effects on both Heybridge and Maldon. Both settlements relied, though not entirely, on the coastal trade for their livelihoods. Most raw materials came by sea, but as more goods were moved in and out of Maldon and Heybridge by rail, so the coastal trade gradually declined. The reduction of coal imports at Heybridge Basin demonstrate this clearly. In 1865, imports amounted to 34,751 tons and in 1885, 10,574 tons. The decline in trade at the Basin was felt in other ways. In 1885, two public houses closed and 12 out of 27 of the Navigation Company's properties were unoccupied. Nevertheless, the depression did not absolutely stifle the development of Maldon or Heybridge. Maldon's population continued to increase from 5,468 in 1881 to 6,559 in 1931 and Heybridge's from 1,677 to 2,061 over the same period. By the 1890s and the later more relaxed Edwardian age, when postcard views became popular, this picturesque area was becoming important for holidaying, bathing and yachting and in 1894 the new Mill Beach Hotel was catering for such visitors. Heybridge Basin became important as a yachting centre and the nearby Blackwater Sailing Club was founded in 1899 by E.H. Bentall.

Maldon, too, was realising its potential as a watering and bathing place and had its Promenade laid out in 1895 and 9,000 people were attracted to the opening of its Marine Lake in 1905. These facilities were clearly aimed at visitors from far away. Victorian and Edwardian Maldon developed physically well beyond its mediaeval limits and Heybridge became more urban in character.

The economic changes of the Victorian and Edwardian periods also brought about social changes. It is noticeable that elementary education figured large with both the religious societies, the National and the British, building and enlarging their schools, but the Literary and Mechanics' Institute of 1841 survived only till 1886. After 1902, the County became involved in education and built a Grammar School in 1907 and elementary schools in Wantz Road in 1911 and at Heybridge in 1913 replacing Heybridge Iron Works School. The established churches were also restored and nonconformist churches were either rebuilt or built anew. In addition a new Roman Catholic church was built.

Piped water, turned on at 6 a.m., and gas, were provided and after 1912 Sadd's supplied electricity to Maldon and Heybridge. Cycles and, later, cars, especially after the First World War, made the population much more mobile. Although there was some unemployment, Maldon was housing an increasing influential and affluent society, some members of which were related to the mills and works of Maldon and Heybridge: but increasingly Maldon was also becoming the residential area for the retired and those who were working outside the town. It was not until 1934 that Heybridge and Mill Beach were included within the Borough of Maldon so no longer was Heybridge just 'a suburb of Maldon' but part of it.

In the pages that follow, an indication is given of some of the social and economic influences that changed the fabric of Maldon and Heybridge between 1880 and 1930.

My grateful thanks to the following for their help: Miss J. Barford, Miss C. Bate, Mrs. M. Binder, Mr. R. Bird, Mrs. J. Cook, Mr. and Mrs. M. Earnshaw, Mr. Victor Gray and Staff at the Essex Record Office, Mr. S. Jarvis and Staff at Chelmsford Central Library, Mrs. V.J. Knightbridge, Dr. A. Knightbridge, Mrs. F. Lucy, Father A. McKintosh, Mrs. E. Mott, Mr. S. Nunn, Dr. W. Petchey, Mr. D. Punchard, Mrs. Richardson, Mrs. G. Shacklock, The Plume Library and Mr. and Mrs. C. Tait. Lastly, to my wife, Wendy, who has completed all the typewriting. Without her help this volume would never have been completed on time.

Maldon Wycke

1. This pastoral scene epitomises the fact that so much of Maldon beyond the built up area was truly rural and this was very true in Victorian and Edwardian times. Maldon Wycke just off the Spital Road is probably a house of seventeenth century date and this is where Mr. Henry Hance, a Maldon merchant, retired to in 1770 where he possessed 'a very handsome house'. In 1777 it is recorded that Mr. Hance *gave for 2 or 3 years a kind of Fete Champaitre; the young folks and most of his neighbours were invited and after tea in the house they danc'd in the barn, where fruit and other refreshments were partook by the company.* Spanning the years from c1890 to the First World War the Wycke was occupied by Miss Mary Staines who was one of the principal landowners in Maldon.

2. A large farmyard surrounded by barns stood to the Maldon side of Spital Farm. In 1913 the dilapidated barns were pulled down to reveal the ruins of St. Giles' Hospital. This leper hospital was founded towards the end of the twelfth century and much of the structure is of that date or slightly later. The hospital was granted to Beeleigh Abbey in 1481 together with 90 acres of land, but with the closure of Beeleigh Abbey the hospital ceased to function and later became a barn. The de-roofed ruins remained in a dangerous state until purchased by Mr. Thomas of Beeleigh Abbey in 1925 who then presented the ruins to the Maldon Corporation. In January 1927, the Corporation commenced work, with direct labour, to restore the ruins and work was completed on 3 June 1927. It is difficult to realise that the hospital ruins were beneath this huge barn.

3. A zeppelin raid on Maldon in 1915 completely destroyed Arthur Smith's brick built workshop next to Rose Cottage in Spital Road. Arthur Smith was a builder, but fortunately his home was at 17 Spital Road closer to the town. Here the photograph shows many interested spectators kept at bay by soldiers and Mr. Thomas Bate, cycle maker and member of the local volunteers, standing with his fixed bayonet. In the distance can be seen the buildings of William S. Markham, aerated water manufacturer. The weather boarded Rose Cottage is probably of eighteenth century date. Between that and the large tree can be seen the cupola of Maldon Grammar School built in 1907.

4. The Union House, complete with workhouse, infirmary, hospital and chapel 'stands in a commanding position and is quite an ornament to the town'. It was built in 1873 at the cost of £21,500 by Mr. Ebenezer Saunders, a local builder, from plans by Mr. Frederick Peck. The premises cover five acres and the house was calculated to hold 350 inmates. The Union House was operated by the Board of Guardians of the Poor, but in 1929 the Guardians were dissolved and the relief of the poor became a County responsibility. Until then the Union had covered 36 local parishes. In 1899 Charles Timperly was master, Reverend T.L. Pearson, who previously had been the master of Maldon Grammar School, 1870-1895, chaplain, and Dr. Thomas Tomlinson of 24 High Street was surgeon and medical officer. This view shows the neo-Tudor Union building, centre, and the chapel on the right.

Spital Villas, Maldon.

5. In this view of Spital Road c1905 the cows on the right are emerging from Ware Pond. Spital Villas, right, were built in the late 1870s on what was orchard land. The six bar gate shown led into 2 Spital Road which in 1900 was owned by Joseph Payne, coachbuilder, 'where new and secondhand vehicles of all descriptions are exposed for sale'. The notice near the gate advertises: 'Traps for Hire.' Later these premises were taken over by Clifford Thomas Orth, coachbuilder, who also kept the horses which pulled the wooden fire engine that was then kept in London Road. Out of the sixteen Spital Villas eight occupants regarded themselves as 'Private Residents' in 1899. On the extreme left, can be seen parts of 3 and 5 Spital Road. Number 5 is where Mr. T.S. Bate the cycle maker and racer had his Eureka works in c1876 and later these premises were taken over by Mr. John Gozzett, builder, who was there in the 1890s.

6. Coronation celebrations 21 June 1911, viewed at the top of the High Street. Following services in the town's churches and a 21 gun salute and feu de joie on the Grammar School Field, at 2 o'clock a parade of decorated carriages, motor cars, trade carts, cycles and tableaux on trolleys was judged in London Road. The Maldon Town Band then led a procession comprising the G. Company of the Essex 5th Regiment, here assembled, the 1st Maldon Company Boys Brigade, Scouts, Fire Brigade and the decorated vehicles down the High Street to Mill Road and the Promenade. In the evening there were celebrations with fireworks; and a torchlight procession wound its way up Mill Road and the High Street to a bonfire on Tyler's Hill at what is now the top of St. Giles' Crescent. The site of the proposed police station is on the right.

7. The original Moot Hall is shown on the extreme left. Silver Street leads through what was the Fish Market in the middle ages. The Blue Boar takes its sign (boar=verres) from the heraldic device of the de Veres, the Earls of Oxford, who owned this site in the middle ages. Behind the white brick front of c1800 and through the arch there is some magnificent timber construction of the fourteenth and fifteenth centuries. At the turn of the century this was one of the two principal inns in Maldon and was kept by Mrs. Sarah Elizabeth Hickford. The inn was then described as 'a commercial hotel and posting house; hearse and mourning coaches for hire' and in 1894 'omnibus attends trains', one of which is standing in the street. Behind the trees is All Saints' church tower which is of thirteenth century date and triangular in plan, a shape unique in this country.

Golf Links, Maldon.

8. This enormous viaduct photographed c1900 was constructed to take the new railway line from Maldon East to Maldon West which then linked Maldon directly with Woodham Ferrers and London via Shenfield. The idea was to have a through service from Colchester to Southend via Maldon but this was never a successful venture. The huge embankments were made of waste from London and very good specimens of pots and bottles thrown out as rubbish by Londoners are buried here. The line was opened 30 September 1889. In the distance can be seen the golf course which was laid out by Thompson of Felixstowe in 1881. The course comprised 9 holes of 2,189 yards. In 1900 there was a club house and there were fifty members each paying a yearly subscribtion of 10s 6d. The president of the club was Reverend E.R. Horwood, vicar of All Saints, and the secretary was Mr. E.E. Bentall of Heybridge.

9. This was what the east front of Beeleigh Abbey looked like c1900. Until 1920 the Abbey was owned by the Baker family of Hockley. The building remained in a rather dilapidated state until in 1912 a lease was granted to Captain F.W. Grantham who set about restoring the Abbey and to erect a range of domestic buildings. This scheme was entrusted to Mr. Basil Ionides under whose supervision the work was sympathetically carried out. In 1920 the Abbey and its immediate surroundings were sold to Jessie Harriette, wife of Richard Edwin Thomas, and in 1943 the property came into the hands of Mr. W. Foyle.

Beeleigh Abbey, MALDON.

10. Beeleigh Abbey c1905. This was founded for Premonstratensian monks by Robert Mantell, Lord of the Manor of Little Maldon, in 1180. These white monks, so called because of their white habits, were puritans among the canons regular. They lived as communities of priests observing a discipline and living a common life. Beeleigh Abbey was dissolved in 1536 and in 1540 the Abbey and much of its land was sold to Sir John Gate of High Easter for £300. All that remained of the Abbey was the east wing of the cloister containing the Chapter House and Calefactory or warming house. The timbered wing, right, was added after the Reformation and the wing, left, was fashioned out of the remains of the Abbey. The buildings, extreme left, undoubtedly mark the site of the west cloister range. The Abbey's water supply would have been as shown; the water from a spring in Beeleigh Fields.

Lion Avenue, Maldon.

11. As you pass through a five bar gate into the grounds of Beeleigh Falls House a Gothic cottage is passed on your right. Almost immediately opposite the cottage stood a remarkable elm which had developed an excrescence resembling that of the head of a lion. This was referred to as the 'Lion Tree' hence the name Lion Avenue was given to this beautiful tree lined walk which was an appropriate access to the local beauty spot of Beeleigh. This view of c1910 shows the Lion Tree and the well trimmed avenue. Following the First World War the tree was decapitated at a point immediately above the head and was finally removed c1934. At the turn of the century this property, Beeleigh Falls House, was owned by Henry Ward, Esquire, a Justice of the Peace of the Borough, whose father had taken over Beeleigh Mill in 1834. In 1835 and 1836 Beeleigh had its own cricket team.

12. This mill at Beeleigh, built in 1797, was on the site of yet older mills going back to Domesday. Arthur Young, Secretary of the Board of Agriculture, waxed eloquently about this mill. *The wheel is twenty four feet in diameter... all the barges come under the mill for loading and unloading, the sacks drawn up or let down with great expedition and all machinery and contrivances for abridging labour appear to be disposed to much perfection. The residence, cottages and the environs form a picturesque and very agreeable scenery.* In 1845 a Wentworth Beam engine was installed in the building, left, with the tall chimney. When the mill was burned down on 12 March 1875, it had 17 pairs of stones, 12 of them worked by water. Only the lower walls and the barge loading bays of the water mill remain and even the head water, shown here, was filled in during the 1960s.

Beeleigh Weir and Lock.

13. Beeleigh Weir and Lock c1905. Although this area of water is not actually in Maldon, Beeleigh has been frequented by Maldonians for afternoon walks and rambles from mid-Victorian times onwards. The area of water shown here is an artificial cut, made for the Chelmer and Blackwater Navigation in 1793, which linked together those two rivers. Contained within the cut is Beeleigh Lock which enables barges to make an ascent or descent of 5 feet 10 inches. On the left is Beeleigh Weir which took the excess waters of the River Blackwater that flowed in from the right, yet retained sufficient depth of water for barges to pass to and from Heybridge Basin. The rustic structure across the weir, to accommodate the horses pulling the barges, constructed in c1793 and greatly repaired in 1842, was swept away in the winter floods of 1947.

Beeleigh Falls, MALDON

14. The tide creeps in silently to this pool at the base of Beeleigh Falls thirteen miles or more from the open sea. Hope Moncrieff, 1909, wrote that one comes 'to a pretty spot where the Chelmer rushes into the Blackwater by 'falls' that if not rivalling Niagara, seem as unique in Essex as the triangular spire (sic) of Maldon is in England'. Indeed until the 1960s when self acting weirs were added to prevent flooding this 13 foot fall of water was a spectacular sight during flood time. The falls took all the excess water from the Chelmer that was not required by Beeleigh Mill. Even here in this photograph of c1904 the extensive frost has not absolutely stopped the force of the water.

Lodge Road, Maldon.

15. Lodge Road was a fashionable, but very private road that was developed during the late Victorian and the Edwardian period and numbers 6 and 8 were already built by 1895. This road ran to a house called 'The Lodge' which had been built in 1807 and used as a barracks. Later it was converted into a house. Eventually houses were built along this road on the very edge of what was then the built up area of Maldon. The houses occupied one of the best prospects in Maldon with spectacular views over towards Beeleigh and to the heights of Wickham Bishops. By 1902 Percy Munro Beaumont, civil engineer, architect and surveyor, was living at Danescroft and by 1908 Reverend Thomas Alexander, Congregational Minister, was living at Number 10 which was finally purchased as The Manse on 5 April 1933. Miss Marion Bradbury was keeping a Preparatory School at Number 2 and by 1922 Mr. Sydney Isaacs was running a boys' school at Numbers 6 and 8.

Grammar School, London Road, Maldon.

16. Maldon Grammar School had several 'homes' in the town. This one in London Road, shown left, was the penultimate and was occupied by the 1880s. School was held in a small, damp, cold room behind the house. Reverend Thomas Layton Pearson was master and he coupled this post with that of chaplain to the Union. During his mastership Reverend Pearson became crippled with rheumatism but continued as chaplain to the Union after his retirement. By 1895, when Reverend Ryland was appointed, there were only five boys and the school was so badly equipped 'that when artificial light was required the pupils had to bring a candle and balance it upon their desks' (W. Petchey). Reverend Ryland did wonders for the school and within two years of his appointment the roll had increased to 42. Reverend Ryland resigned a year before the new school was opened in Fambridge Road in 1907. On the right can be seen the gable of the National (C. of E.) Schools, opened in 1847, which had cost £1,500 to build.

LONDON ROAD MALDON

17. Long before the turn of the century the Maldon Borough Fire Brigade had been established in London Road at the premises shown here c1905 with the glass doors to the street and the look out tower on the roof. This is where the steam and manual fire engines and fire escape were kept. In the event of fire the hour bell at the Moot Hall served the purpose as a fire alarm, but after c1909 the firemen were alerted by a telephone system. The fire alarm having been given the first fireman on duty had to go to Mr. Orth at 2 Spital Road, to fetch the horses. In 1890 J.W. Hawkes was the Captain and he had a full time occupation as a plumber and he lived at 28 High Street, but by 1899 he was resident on the spot at 20 London Road, and so were his successors. The Town's Museum was once housed in a room above the Fire Station. In the distance right, is Maldon Grammar School. This end of the weather boarded cottages was occupied by Mr. Henry Balls, tailor.

18. This view shows the High Street c1905. The researches of Dr. W. Petchey have now made us more aware of the reasons behind the widening of the High Street at this point. The original Moot Hall was the building here occupied by Dibben and Son; on the right in front of All Saints' Church is shown the row of shops pulled down in 1917. This row extended even further west, but three shops were burned down in 1858. Originally a narrow row of shops stood in the middle of the street and stretched from the King's Head to Silver Street. It was the Shambles or Butchers' Row which was pulled down in 1639. The narrow street to its right was the Mercers' Lane and that to its left was the Corn Market. The 'Garage' shown left must have been one of the earliest in Maldon. In 1906 it was advertised as 'Bates Cycle and Motor Works, cycle manufacturers'.

Gowers, Ltd., Maldon.

19. All Saints' Church, c1900. Its thirteenth century triangular tower and hexagonal spire are unique. This south side of the church is now open to the High Street. The western half of this aisle was built c1330 and is one of the best examples of early fourteenth century architecture in Essex. Then in the mid-fifteenth century Sir Robert D'Arcy added three bays to the east to accommodate his chantry where priests said masses for the souls of his family. Alterations were made to this elevation with the provision of statues for the niches in 1907 and the square headed door was replaced with one of Gothic design in 1920. It was presented by the late Miss Warren and designed by Wykeham Chancellor, MA. Lawrence Washington, the great-great-grandfather of George Washington, was buried in this churchyard on 21 January 1652. A new 'Washington window', to the right of the door, was presented in 1928 by the citizens of Malden, Massachusetts.

Maldon. All Saints' Church

20. The hall like appearance was given to All Saints in 1728 when the north aisle and nave were merged to form a large preaching space. That is why the two prominent eastern arches are of classical appearance. This photograph of c1920 shows many of the alterations made in the Victorian and Edwardian periods. The eagle lectern was presented by the Maldon Freemasons in 1866. The pulpit was erected in 1867 and originally stood on the north side of the chancel, but was moved to this position in 1903. In 1905 the mediaeval rood loft staircase was discovered above the hymn board. The chancel screens, north and south, were erected in 1906 to the designs of P.M. Beaumont, architect, and carved by S. Marshall of Coggeshall. They also did the choir stalls and hymn boards. The Victorian font has a cover inscribed: *The gift of the Sunday Catechism, A.D. 1902.*

21. All Saints' Vicarage. This attractive house was probably built under the will of Sir Robert D'Arcy (1385-1448) to house the priests who sung masses for the souls of the D'Arcy family, and others, in his newly founded Chantry Chapel in All Saints' Church. The house was altered in the seventeenth century when the centre roof was raised to the level of the two gables. Reverend Edward Russell Horwood, MA, was vicar here from 1850 to 1901. He was most influential in the Borough as a Magistrate, Plume Librarian, Member of the Burial Board and Board of Guardians, an Income and Land Tax Commissioner and was president of the golf, cricket, lawn tennis and rowing clubs and Philharmonic Society. He also presided over the Easter Dinners, attended by Townsmen of all denominations, for 49 years. An altogether ecumenical outlook for a high churchman of those days. Reverend Horwood was followed by Reverend A. Wilson, MA, in 1901 and in 1903 by Reverend Leonard Hughes, MA, BD, who wrote an excellent guide to All Saints' Church in 1909.

22. *The cottages which hide the south aisle from the street are obvious encroachments and their removal is a consummation devoutly to be wished,* so wrote Reverend Leonard Hughes, vicar of All Saints, in 1909. Their removal was achieved in 1917. This row formerly extended even further west, but three shops were burned down in 1858. From left to right the shops down as far as the Moot Hall formed an interesting assemblage of businesses c1907. Victor Brock, confectioner, occupied 27; Spurgeon and Son, auctioneers, valuers and estate agents with John Elgar Bonner, dentist and artificial teeth maker, above, at 29; Lewis Volta, confectioner and ice cream maker, at 31 and Arthur French, fishmonger, at 33. Beyond Church Walk the shops were occupied as follows; The London Central Meat Company Ltd., with John Guiver, insurance agent, above, at 35; Richard Poole, printer, bookseller and stationer, at 37; and Wade Brothers, butchers, at 39. These shops certainly gave the Market Place confinement and a rather quaint air.

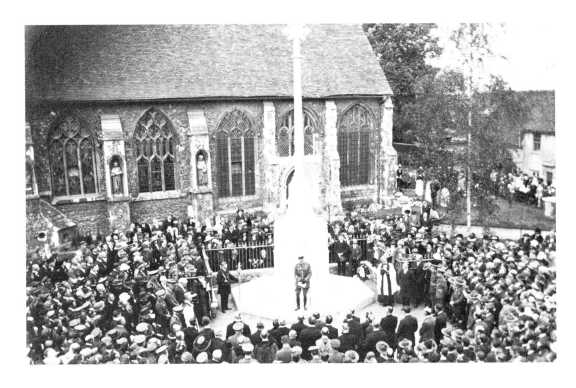

23. Maldon War Memorial was dedicated on Sunday 8 May 1921, when the Market Square and High Street were thronged with people and All Saints' bells rang out a muffled peal. The memorial of Portland Stone, bearing 146 names, was designed by Wykeham Chancellor, MA, and was carved and erected by Wray and Fuller of Chelmsford. Here General Horne is speaking after the unveiling ceremony. To his left is the Mace Bearer; the Mayor, Councillor H.W. Sadd, JP; the Town Clerk; and the Bishop of Barking who dedicated the memorial. To General Horne's right is Reverend I.L. Seymour, vicar of All Saints. Over 300 ex-service-men, under the command of Admiral Kennedy, and the Scouts formed a cordon around the memorial. In front of General Horne are many dignitaries including the Mayor and Mayoress of Chelmsford; the Mayor and Mayoress of Colchester; Sir Fortescue and Lady Flannery; Sir Claude and Lady de Crespigney; General Sir S.W. Hare; General Da Costa; and many others.

High Street, Maldon.

24. The Moot Hall was built early in the fifteenth century by Sir Robert D'Arcy. It became the property of the Borough in 1576 when it was bought for £55 from Thomas Eve, alderman and linen draper. Its present front elevation and portico (rails added to this c1905) are the result of a restoration of c1811. Until c1914 part of the ground floor was the police station, complete with prison cells. The first floor was a court, a reminder that Maldon once held its own Quarter Sessions and other courts. The Borough Council met until 1974 in the room above the clock. In 1884 the building received a considerable shock from the Essex earthquake. Head Constable Wombwell and PC Parrott were so alarmed by a great crash at the back of the building that they thought the whole place was falling about their ears and ran into the High Street only to see hosts of other people there also. The crash was caused by the violent colliding of the weights of the town clock.

25. This part of the clock is not easily seen from the street. George Courtauld, the last MP for the Borough, presented both a public clock and chimes in 1881. The work was carried out by Gillett and Bland of Croydon. The chime comprises four bells: the heaviest weighing nearly 6¼ hundredweight and the lightest over 2¼ hundredweight. The hour bell weighs just over 7½ hundredweight. The music of the chimes was composed by Dr. Crotch and comprises a phrase from the fifth bar in the opening symphony of Handel's air 'I know that my Redeemer liveth'. The clock was started on Thursday 20 October 1881, by the Mayor, Mr. J.G. Sadd, and its donor expressed the wish that as the clock's hours pass by ...*they will find this borough still in the enjoyment of its prosperity and may find the inhabitants of this borough still in the enjoyment of the happiness, peace and comfort which I am sure they all deserve!*

26. A large number of people had gathered in the High Street to witness this solemn procession which had assembled at 12.45 p.m. at the Moot Hall prior to a service at All Saints for the funeral of King Edward VII on 20 May 1910. The procession comprised the Police, the Town Band playing the 'Dead March in Saul', The Mayor, Deputy Mayor, Aldermen, Magistrates, Councillors, Borough Officials, Fire Brigade and Territorials, led by the Mace Bearer draped in black crepe. The service was equally fitted to the occasion commencing with the hymn 'When our heads are bow'd with woe'. During the morning the bells of All Saints had rung out a solemn deep muffled 2¾ hour peal of 5,040 changes. The ringers were: W. Chalk, senior, A. Mansfield, W.G. Mansfield, A. Gozzett, H.J. Mansfield (conductor) and T. Chalk. Also shown here is the row of five shops, demolished in 1917, with Mr. Volta's flag flying at half mast.

27. The King's Head dates from the early sixteenth century when it comprised a cross wing on the left and a large two storey open hall in the centre. It was altered in the eighteenth century when the 'hall' was divided horizontally and a new cross wing built on the right. At this time the whole of the front was bricked and refenestrated. It was owned by Jonas and Rachel Malden and in 1744 they sold it to Joseph Pattisson. In 1732 it is described as *a large and commodious House with Stables, Coach House ... situated in the best part of the town.* During the building of the Chelmer and Blackwater Navigation, 1793-1797, John Rennie, FRS, the famous Canal engineer, stayed here the few times he visited the site. In 1900 the hotel was owned by Mr. J.H. Taylor who was 'a good host' and excellent caterer. Guests were met from the station by the carriage shown. The hotel was the meeting place of the Maldon Cycle Club.

High Street, Maldon.

28. Cows in Maldon High Street c1900. Cows were milked in one of the High Street yards, perhaps at Alfred Lucking's, he was a farmer and cattle dealer at No 100, and then driven out to fields in London Road and Spital Road. The Chequers, right, kept by Elijah Young is advertising 'The Colchester Brewing Co's Fine Old Ales'. Beyond Friar's Lane is a draper's shop, No 62, kept by Alfred Bailey and later taken over by Alfred Hardy-King and Company. The next shop No 64 was that of Arthur Heaver, chemist and druggist, later Alfred Appleby, bootmaker; No 66 was later occupied by Thomas Turner, clothier; No 68 by Caleb and Samuel Finch, watchmakers, and No 70 by Alfred Clear, auctioneer, valuer and estate agent, and was later the residence of Dr. Henry Reynolds Brown. The Swan in the background, left, had not been refronted when this view was taken.

Maldon. High Street.

29. 'The thousands of spectators who witnessed the burning pile will never forget the sight' of the fire on the night of Sunday 17 January 1892. The fire started beneath a staircase in Orttewell's ironmongers and spread up the High Street to Marrison's, bootmakers, the Misses Thompson, dressmakers, and Mr. Frederick Green's. The fire also spread down the High Street to Mrs. Andrews, jewellers, to Mr. Rudkin, tobacconist, and Mr. Fuller, bootmaker. Mr. Archer's draper's shop on the corner was saved but two shops on Market Hill owned by Mr. Croft, tailor, and Mr. Hayes, wine and spirit merchant, sustained damage. Most of the shops were rebuilt in either 1892 or 1893 but two sites were left vacant as is shown here and the 'new' Post Office was slotted into this space c1907. During the fire the Post Office, then on the opposite side of the street, and other shops 'were much scorched and blistered and some panes of glass broken by the heat'.

30. The Bate Cycle Company Limited c1900. Thomas Bate, standing outside his shop on Market Hill, started making cycles in the late 1870s at his Eureka Works in Spital Road. He left Maldon but returned to take up this site. His advertisement makes interesting reading. The Company *invite inspection by a critical public of their superb specimens of Cycle Construction; a variety of models to suit the tourist of either sex who desires class and comfort or the speed man who yearns to break records or to win prizes, but one quality only; the Best 'BATES UNIQUE' CYCLES.* His advertisment continues *Riding taught by competent Instructors. We keep a large stock of Reliable Cycles to LET or HIRE.* The shop next door was then kept by Thomas Hayes, Railway Receiving Office, who was a wholesale wine and spirit merchant; he later moved from 3 to 11 Market Hill.

Market Hill, Maldon

31. In the middle ages this part of Market Hill, photographed c1920, was called St. Peter's Lane (W. Petchey). Percy Daniels' draper's shop on the extreme left was rebuilt after a fire of 1882. The Maldon Cycle Company (originally The Bate Cycle Company) manifested its trade by the huge 'penny' wheel projecting from its gable. The next shop was once a butchers kept by Mr. Farley. The next two shops were pulled down to make way for the Jubilee Hall c1923 and the next shop with its first floor bay was kept by William Hayes, wine and spirit merchant. That brings us to the corner of Bull Lane; on the other side of this lane is shown a large, square, three storey building that was owned by the Maldon and Heybridge Co-operative Society which was selling all sorts of groceries, boots, shoes and drapery. The wall of St. Peter's churchyard, right, was set back 13 feet 6 inches in 1926 because it was an obstruction to traffic.

St Peters Maldon

32. St. Peter's Church had become redundant in the middle ages and by 1665 the nave had collapsed. Interest in this site was shown by Dr. Thomas Plume who had been born in Maldon in 1630 and educated at Chelmsford Grammar School and Christ's College, Cambridge. In 1658 he was appointed vicar of Greenwhich and in 1679 he became Archdeacon of Rochester an office he held until his death in 1704. Before his death, however, Dr. Plume had erected a red brick building on the site of the old nave c1699 to house a library upstairs and a school downstairs. Moreover, he restored the old mediaeval tower of St. Peter's. Unfortunately, by c1900 the tower had become so unsafe at the top that it had to have a band put around it as shown here to hold it together. In 1930 when Mr. E.T. Baker, JP, was Chairman of the Plume Trustees, the tower was restored by Mr. Frank Sherling, a local builder.

33. The interior of The Plume Library before 1925. The Library was originally built five bays long but it was extended another two bays in 1817 when the National School was founded and occupied the ground floor. The Grammar School was ousted, but returned in the 1850s to occupy the end of the Library for a few years. This shows well some of the enormous bookshelves made, before Dr. Plume died, to accommodate the 7,000 or so volumes which he willed to his native town. In modern terms of subject matter they include several main categories from Mathematics to Theology and from Medicine to Classical Languages. In age the volumes range from late fifteenth century to 1704. As Dr. Petchey has pointed out this library was not so much Dr. Plume's personal working collection (though his volumes are included) but an attempt at a general reference library. The gas mantle was replaced with electricity in 1925 and the marble fire surround with wood in 1927.

Maldon.   *Congregational Church.*

34. This Congregational Church was erected between 1800 and 1801 on the site of a previous church. It was opened in July 1801, by the then pastor Mr. Foster and had cost about £3,000. It was given a new front c1860. At the turn of the century its pastor was Reverend H. Herman Carlisle, MA. It was he who erected new buildings adjoining the old British Schools (part shown left) which comprised classrooms for day and Sunday Schools and a spacious Lecture Hall all costing £2,000. The church had seats for 950 people and in 1899 there were two services on Sunday and one on Thursday. The British Schools closed when the Wantz Road Schools opened in 1911. The nineteenth and early twentieth century graveyard monuments to the north of the church are very interesting and indicate the close links between business and Nonconformity in the Maldon area. The conspicious tomb in the foreground probably belongs to the Bourne family of Mundon and was removed c1965.

Maldon. Hill House.

35. This magnificent piece of architecture, Hill House, with its prominent belvedere, was built by the Sadd family in the early nineteenth century. By the 1880s it was occupied by Alfred Granger Sadd (1829-1902), a director of John Sadd and Sons Limited, timber importers and builders' merchants and one of the leading firms in Maldon. From the early part of this century Hill House was occupied by Miss Henrietta Sadd (1863-1932) who founded the 'Home of Rest for Young Women' which was housed in the weather boarded house shown on the left. This home, and another owned by Miss Sadd in Wantz Road, was set aside for women who could not otherwise afford a holiday or who were convalescing from an illness such as tuberculosis. Some of the employees of Bryant and May's Match Works stayed here. Hill House was left to the Borough of Maldon and in 1937 it became the Municipal Offices of the town. In 1974 it was taken over by the new Maldon District Council and in 1985 it was up for sale.

Maldon, Market Hill.

36. In the middle ages this part of the hill was called Fullbridge Street (W. Petchey). Being the only connection between the north of the river and the town it was well used. A number of shops and houses, right, are of mediaeval or later date. The first is advertising 'Lyons Tea' and the shop below with a sign was Blaxall's, the butcher. Hillside, left, was built as the Union Workhouse c1836 but ceased to serve that function with the opening of the Maldon Union Workhouse (St. Peter's Hospital) in 1873. It was then divided into tenements and for twenty years or more down to 1914 part of it was a girls' school kept by Miss Kate Cromar. Notice the gravel surfaced road c1905 and the elegant looking lady pushing her cycle down the hill probably, because, as Fitch had commented, in c1895 that this hill was 'one of the most dangerous for bicyclists in the country'.

Maldon.   Hill Side.

37. Market Hill, pre-1905. The iron bridge across the River Chelmer was built in 1877 for £4,000 and rebuilt in 1961. On the left going up the hill were the following properties: Rutt Gutteridge and Company corn, coal and lime merchants; Joseph Gripper, ironmonger; a furniture shop; James Crowe, fruiterer; The Customs House; Brown the butcher; and Argent the fruiterer. Beyond the boarded cottages on the right was F. Luckin Smith, grocer at 49 and then The Ship Inn advertising 'Salt's Burton Ales' and 'Good Stabling'. It was at this inn that those gentlemen who were not engaged in the game of cricket on Potman Marsh '...staid at the Ship smok'd their pipes and played a game of cards' in the 1780s. The fourth shop down on the left was kept by Robert Blaxall, butcher and one time Borough Councillor.

Maldon : The Wharf

38. This is the tidal River Chelmer from Fullbridge c1910. On the left a barge is drawn up at Mr. E.T. Baker's roller mill where wheat was ground into flour for the London market. This building was put up in 1878 by Bentall Bros. as a nut and bolt factory. The white building, left, is on Rayleigh Wharf, so called because it was owned by the Strutt family, MPs for Maldon, who later took the title of Rayleigh. Samuel Garrett who had been at Hoe Mill since c1865 built a new steam roller mill here c1895 where it was much easier to import wheat and barge sacks of flour to the London market. In the distance, left, can be seen the wharfs and sheds of John Sadd and Sons, Ltd., English and foreign timber and builders' merchants. On the right is Fullbridge Wharf where Rutt, Gutteridge and Co, Ltd., corn, coal and seed merchants, had a lime kiln.

Fullbridge Street, Maldon.

39. Fullbridge looking towards the bridge c1906. The large house here, known as Rivercourt, was obviously an old building which had been refronted sometime in the eighteenth century. This house was occupied by Miss Henderson in 1912, but during the First World War it was commandeered and was used by the Red Cross for troops who were convalescing. Following the war Rivercourt was occupied by Miss Short who took in boarders from the Grammar School. The building, extreme left, was the Welcome Sailor kept by Alfred Crabbe and next door, with a large lamp outside, was the White Hart kept in 1912 by George Sewell. Also in that year Arthur Dykes, earthenware dealer, occupied the house this side of the White Hart.

Maldon East Station

40. Maldon East Station must have been one of the finest railway stations in the whole country. It was built in 1848 as part of the Maldon, Witham and Braintree Railway in the Jacobean style in red and white brick. Maldon owes its oppulent station to Mr. David Waddington, an Eastern Counties Director, who was candidate for the Borough; his employees, called 'guinea pigs', had to be kept in residence much longer than anticipated in order to increase Mr. Waddington's chances of election as the Borough's Liberal MP. In the 1890s Liverpool Street, 44 miles, could be reached for 11s and 3s 3½d first and third class returns respectively. There were eight trains on weekdays and three on Sundays via Witham. The King's Head carriage is waiting for the arrival of a train to take guests to Maldon in this view of c1910.

41. Maldon East Station must have been a busy place when this photograph was taken c1911. It was necessary to keep ample staff to deal with the eight passengers trains a day and also to deal with the goods that came to the station for despatch to London. The principal trade was in vegetables and other agricultural produce, such as blackcurrants, for Stratford Market, which is mentioned on a poster in the background. The characters in this photograph from left to right are, back row: Unknown, counter hand for Smith's book stall; Mr. Boreham, porter; F.W. Pyke, signalman; Fred Bowles, horse and cart delivery; Bob Kettle, passenger guard; and man standing, Unknown, was the booking clerk. In the front row: Ernest Bowles, signalman from 1935 to 1949; Unknown, relief signalman; Frederick Blyth, station master; Adam Eve, porter; Unknown, relief signalman; and Alfred Alders, shunter. (Characters have been identified by Mr. F. Pyke, aged 90.) All activities at the station ceased after the closure of the line to Witham in 1966. The station building has now been turned into the Great Eastern Motel and public house.

42. This view of the High Street c1912 shows Church House, extreme left, which was the home of Edward Bright who died in 1750 at the age of 29 and weighed 44 stones. This house was occupied at the turn of the century by the Bentall family, drapers in the town, and by 1912 it had come into the hands of Leonard Bentall who was Mayor of the Borough in 1890 and 1895. The row of three shops, with their blinds, belonged to the Hicks family. Lewis D. Hicks occupied the first two with his ironmongery and cycle agents businesses. The last of the three shops was owned by Charles H. Hicks who was a corn merchant and seedsman. The tricycle ridden by the boy is owned by Hicks. The Swan, an ancient house refronted, was occupied in 1899 by William Head and in 1912 by Henry Charles William Conn. The bow windowed house, extreme right, was occupied by Dr. Henry Reynolds Brown, surgeon and medical officer of health to the Corporation.

HIGH STREET, MALDON.

43. This is the lower part of the High Street c1914. At the end of the row of shops, left, can be seen the gable and canopy of The Hippodrome Picture Palace. This was opened c1910 and in 1911 it was advertising a 'Splendid Series of Incomparable Electric Pictures changed every Monday and Thursday' and commencing 11 December was the following with comments in brackets: 'Carmenita, The Faithful (splendid drama); Beaux Not Wanted (funny); Mystery of the Lonely Gulch (thrilling); A Child's Judgement (very pathetic); The Regeneration (a fine drama); The Act of Paying One's Debts (roars).' Seats 4d, 6d or 9d, children half price. Between the left hand edge of this view and the cinema in 1912 there were shops purveying the following goods or services: a hair dresser, a fruiterer, a draper and an oilman.

High Street Maldon *Wesleyan Church Maldon* Gowers Ltd. Maldon 354

44. The High Street c1905 shows, left, The Trees and immediately opposite, right, a huge four storey building of c1890 which housed the business of Jeffrey's and Sons, clothiers, 127 High Street, who later took over 129 and 131. The latter had previously been occupied c1900 by George Finch, pork butcher, and in 133 he also carried on the business of plumber and glazier. The shop next to the church was occupied in 1900 by Samuel Lewin, baker. Methodism first put down its roots in Maldon in 1753 opposite this church in a house called 'Cat's Castle' which owed its name to an eccentric lady who wanted to own 21 cats but was always thwarted in her quest. In 1824 a small chapel (now the Labour Hall) was built in Church Street. The church shown here was built in 1861 by Thomas King of Maldon to the designs of James Moore of Great Totham at a cost of £973.

45. The Trees, formerly Holly Trees, Hardings, and before that Spencers, stood on the corner of Wantz Road where Kathleen's Kitchen now stands. It was said to have been built in Elizabethan times and was remodelled in the early nineteenth century. In the eighteenth century it was occupied by the famous Coe merchant family of the town; in the nineteenth century by George May, surgeon, and then by Mrs. Bell. From 1904 to 1934 it was the home of Mr. E.T. Baker (1869-1948) owner of Fullbridge Mill who was churchwarden of All Saints; a Justice of the Peace for both the Borough and the County, a unique position in those days; and Mayor of Maldon on three occasions 1916-1919, 1921-1922 and 1932-1934. When The Trees was pulled down in 1935 its linenfold panelling, which was emblazoned with the mulet, the de Vere star, was sent to America. In the background, right, can be seen the Primitive Methodist Church built in 1860 and now used by the Salvation Army.

46. Within a quarter of a century of this view of c1905 being taken the Wantz Road corner was to change out of all recognition. The Trees on the corner, left, was pulled down in 1935 and the block of three shops on the opposite corner was gutted by a terrible fire during the night of 14 January 1910. Henry Salter Nalson occupied the grocer's shop designated F. Wigginton. The next shop, 124 High Street, was kept by Mr. C. Parsons, clothier, and 122 High Street was occupied by Mr. William Firmin, butcher. The fire broke out at 2 a.m. in Mr. Parson's kitchen and soon spread to the shops either side. Mr. Firmin's four young children, three girls and a boy, had to be rescued from an upstair window with a ladder by a neighbour from across the road. PC Burrows telephoned the Fire Brigade which was soon on the scene with Captain Tydeman and Sub-captain Pannifer in charge. Water had to be obtained from Dr. Brown's pond and from Mr. E.T. Baker's pond at The Trees.

Wantz Road, Maldon.

47. Wantz Road, nearly a half a mile long, was described in c1895 as 'an important thoroughfare'. Indeed, its importance is manifested in the number of businesses, shops and other services in this road in 1899. It contained a baker, a bootmaker, two beer retailers; a builder; a coal merchant; a fruiterer, two grocers (one running a post office), a pork butcher, a plumber and glazier, a music seller, five shopkeepers, a steam mill, a tailor, The Registrar of Births, Deaths and Marriages, a Methodist Church, the Wantz Brewery, operated by John Hutley, advertising 'Good Sound Hay and Harvest Beers' and four public houses: the Volunteer, the Three Cups, the Star, whose sign can be discerned on the left squeezed between the two tallest blocks of houses, and the Borough Arms, operated by G. Markham, who also manufactured aerated water. This 1905 view was taken about 60 yards north of Dyer's Road.

48. On 30 September 1869, the Essex Baptist Union decided to attempt work in Maldon. In 1870 services were held in the Public Hall and by 1872 the Baptist Congregation had erected a corrugated iron structure in Butt Lane on this site. Several pastors, Mr. Chapman, Mr. Stockdale, Mr. Charlton and Mr. Ernest Cole all worked hard for the Baptist Movement in Maldon. Reverend F.C. Morris was appointed in September 1892, and through his efforts foundation stones were laid by Leonard Bentall, Mayor; Reverend F.C. Morris; Thomas Sadler; and Alderman Joseph Sadler on 1 July 1896, and the chapel was opened on 25 November 1896. It was designed by Mr. P.M. Beaumont, a local architect, and built by A. Baxter and Son at a cost of £1,821:10s:7½d. School rooms were later added at the rear of the chapel to the designs of Mr. Hoyne, architect, and built by A. Ward and Son of Great Totham at a cost of £766:10s. This extension was officially opened in October 1914.

49. A Catholic Chapel was erected in 1897 in Victoria Road and dedicated to the Assumption of Our Lady. This is the stock brick and slated building, now used as the Church Hall, to the left of the present church. The red brick church with stone dressings was built in 1925 and dedicated to the Assumption of Our Lady by the Bishop of Brentwood on 25 October, in that year. Some of the priests that were here earlier this century became well-known. Reverend Adrian Fortescue was a well-known authority on the history of the Greek Church and Father John E. Pettit subsequently became the Bishop of Menevia.

50. Sir Claude de Crespigney, JP, of Great Totham and Aeronaut Simmons had to abandon their balloon trip on 10 June 1882, because of a disastrous take off when Sir Claude broke his leg in two places. The second attempt was on 1 August 1883, and the enormous balloon was inflated in a field near the Gas Works. The balloon was 75 ft in height and 40 ft in diameter and had a capacity of 37,000 cubic feet of gas. Inflating commenced at 5 a.m. and was completed by 11.30 a.m. The car was fixed and made fast to a tree whilst 500lbs of ballast in bags was loaded aboard. At 12.30 p.m. Sir Claude and aeronaut Simmons got under way and successfully landed in Holland. Although this account does not absolutely complement the postcard, because there are no leaves on the trees, this view does show one of Sir Claude's ballooning exploits and the photograph was undoubtedly taken on The Downs.

Hythe Quay, Maldon.

51. The Hythe was owned by the Borough. A map of 1516 shows 'The Townes Colcheape and Chalkheape' and wharfs let to several tenants. This view of c1903 shows the barges being loaded up with hay and straw which was needed for the horse population of London. These barges were loaded very high above the deck line and were referred to as 'stackies'. Locally this barge service to London River was known as 'Hay up and dung down' because the barges returned with London horse muck for spreading on the heavy clay lands adjacent to the banks of the Blackwater Estuary. There were several merchants in Maldon involved in this trade such as Hawes and Thompson 'hay and straw dealer'. In the background can be seen the Queen's Head which was kept by Mrs. Sarah Saunders in 1890 and by Robert Archer in 1899.

52. Although this pre-1886 view fails to show it St. Mary's Church was then in a very bad state of repair. The interior of the church was filled with a forest of dilapidated horsebox pews and only the wealthy could afford to have slow combustion stoves in their pews, the smoke pipes of which poked out through the roof. Indeed the roofs themselves were so bad that they had to be supported by internal posts and other contrivances. It is apparent that the south wall of the Norman nave had been shored up with two enormous brick buttresses. During the restoration of 1886-87 the church was closed for more than a year and it was during this restoration that the chancel arch fell and had to be rebuilt. The church was reopened on Tuesday 29 March 1887, when bunting was hung out for the occasion. The restoration had cost £3,000.

St. Mary's Church, Maldon.

53. St. Mary's stands conspicuously above the estuary. Its foundation is of Saxon date and it was given to St. Martin-le-Grand, London, by Ingelric in 1056. The church was rebuilt c1130 and the north wall of the nave and parts of the chancel arch date from this period. The tower was built c1300, but in the mid-sixteenth century the enormous striped buttress was enlarged to support an ailing upper storey which eventually collapsed in 1598. There was some urgency to rebuild it as the tower 'was a beacon for the river and was causing much inconvenience to navigators'. In spite of this injunction rebuilding was not undertaken until c1635. The shingled spire was built c1740. Apart from the tower and spire this elevation dates from 1886-87. Frederick Chancellor was architect for the nave, aisle and vestry and Ewan Christian architect for the chancel. Henry Gozzett was the builder.

Promenade. Maldon.

2612. 1.

54. As this view demonstrates 26 June 1895, was an important landmark in the provision of recreational facilities in Maldon. This was the day that Maldon was en fete with the opening of the Marine Promenade and Recreation Ground which comprised 14 acres of land laid out with grass, trees and shrubs and costing between £4,000 and £5,000. Every house was decorated for the occasion except for Mr. George Codd's in Silver Street; and as the procession passed his residence the fact that all the blinds were down was made the subject of many jokes; he had not agreed with the scheme. There was a luncheon attended by Mr. George Courtauld, MP, and Mrs. Courtauld and Mr. Cyril Dodd, QC, MP, who observed that 'if young Londoners knew what boating, fishing and bracing air were to be enjoyed at Maldon, Maldon would soon become a London suburb'. The opening was performed by the Mayor and local historian, Mr. Edward A. Fitch, FLA.

Maldon

55. This photograph was taken on 26 June 1895, the day the Marine Promenade and Recreation Ground were opened. It shows the 'Extension' with a band stand half way along. There was also a men's bathing hut at the end. It shows, too, that there were originally two areas of mud and water: one roughly triangular shaped bathing area belonging to the Bath House in the foreground and an oval shaped area in the background. Beyond the oval a creek ran inland to the right of what is now the Lake as far as the bath house (the white house with four chimney pots) which was then occupied by Benjamin T. Handley who let out rowing boats and bathing machines for river bathing. He also kept 'baths' which were probably those hot and cold salt water baths mentioned in the late eighteenth and several times through the nineteenth century. The barge 'Dawn' is in frame between the Bath House and the Thames barge.

Maldon Marine Lake

56. Compared with the previous view of the Marine Lake area this view of c1906 shows the alterations that were made with the formation of the Marine Lake in 1905. The triangular cold water bath belonging to Benjamin Handley's Bath House has disappeared and so has the creek. The oval shaped muddy area which existed before 1905 covered nearly 1½ acres but after the formation of the Marine Lake the area of water covered nearly 2¾ acres. The band stand and the men's bathing hut can easily be seen along the 'Extension'. In addition, the number of boat building sheds has increased and some inhabitants have not given up the idea of river bathing as there are still bathing machines standing by.

Maldon.

57. This shows well the Old Bath Wall before the Marine Lake was formed in 1905. Immediately beyond the first shed the path divided and the left branch went to the Bath House and the other went past the boat yard to the Hythe Quay. The beach at this point was very busy as a barge building area and the Lord Roberts can be seen in building in Cook and Woodard's Yard c1897. Many other craft are moored in the estuary. In the background centre, can be seen the Queen's Head on the Hythe Quay and the road running up to the Castle Inn in North Street. This is really one of the classical views of Maldon with the waterside and St. Mary's conspicuously perched on its hill.

58. The opening of the Marine Lake took place on 23 June 1905. It commenced at the Moot Hall with a procession headed by the Town Band, which included Foresters and Oddfellows, the Volunteers, the Borough Fire Brigade and carriages containing invited guests: the Borough Magistrates, the Corporation and Lord and Lady Rayleigh. There was lunch for the guests in a marquee where appropriate speeches were made. Lady Rayleigh, who formally opened the Marine Lake by turning the handle of the sluice to let in the water, said: 'I have much pleasure in declaring this beautiful lake open.' The Mayor, Lord and Lady Rayleigh and Alderman and Mrs. Fitch then took a trip round the Lake in the Mayor's rowing boat. The construction of the Lake had involved removing 8,000 tons of earth by 35 of the town's unemployed under the supervision of Mr. T.R. Swales, the Borough Engineer. About 9,000 people were present, many of whom had come by rail.

Marine Lake, Maldon.

59. This view of c1908 shows the Bath House which once stood at the head of the creek but subsequently at the end of the Marine Lake. The Corporation paid Benjamin Handley £525 for the Bath Wall property consisting of an extensive open air bathing place enclosed within an embankment: this would have been the roughly triangular area shown in 55. The Bath House was eventually pulled down in the 1930's. This view shows the steep bank of what must have been the edge of the creek here following the path and the new wall running from the Bath House across to the right of the photograph. St. Mary's Church stands poised above the Lake. Its six bells rang out a 2¾hour muffled peal on 20 May 1910, for the funeral of Edward VII. The ringers taking part were: E. Finch, H. Finch, A. South, F. Chalk, A. Gozzett (conductor) and H.J. Mansfield.

The Promenade, Maldon.

60. The Promenade before The Marine Parade widening extensions in 1925 and the Recreation Ground extensions in 1926. On the right can be seen the band stand which was later replaced by a shelter and by 1922 the band stand stood on the steep slope above the Marine Lake. At the end of the Promenade on the left was the men only bathing shed where there was no charge for changing. A small boat with mainsail aloft is just about to leave for a trip down the estuary. In the foreground proud parents push their baby along the Promenade to benefit from the sunshine and fresh air. With more leisure time increasing numbers of day trippers were taking advantage of the Marine Lake and Recreation Ground.

S. S. „Annie" at Landing Stage, Maldon

61. Early this century Osea Island was bought by Mr. F.N. Charrington, the brewer, where he set up a treatment centre for alcoholics. As part of his plan he bought a small steam boat 'S.S. Annie' so that trips could be operated between Maldon and Osea Island where passengers could land or have trips around the Island. Every fortnight there were trips to either Bradwell or West Mersea. At one period they ran moonlight trips, accompanied by banjo music, with lanterns hung in the after awning and on fine nights they presented an idyllic picture and were well patronised by local couples. S.S. Annie operated until 1914 but in 1918 she was refitted with a motorised engine and was then operated as the 'Maldon Annie' until c1920 when she was taken to London River. She was involved in the relief of the Dunkirk beaches but did not return.

Causeway, Maldon.

62. This Causeway viewed in c1905 from the Heybridge end was actually within St. Peter's Parish, Maldon. It united Maldon with Heybridge and was considered so important that Edward II ordered a survey of it in 1324. The Causeway cut right across Potman Marsh 'where in the summer season the gentlemen of Maldon associated into a cricket club, and a regular set played the game' from 1750 to the 1840s. Fairs were also held on the Marsh between 25 and 27 March and on 8 September. Apart from a cluster of houses near Fullbridge, only one or two cottages existed on the Causeway until the late nineteenth and the early twentieth century. Some of these newer houses can be seen together with the lines of trees, which had been planted as an indication of civic pride. On the right can be seen part of the parapet of the mediaeval bridge rebuilt in 1870.

63. This mill stood at the head of Heybridge Creek but the mill was not tidal; it was driven by the water from the Blackwater. For centuries this mill, like much of Heybridge, was owned by the Dean and Chapter of St. Paul's Cathedral. In 1792 the mill was operated by Robert Barnard and in the 1820s by T.R. Webb. By the 1830s it was operated by George Gepp Ward who was there until c1885 when it was taken over by Frederick Cocks, an avowed Congregationalist, who was the miller until c1908. It was he who supplemented water with steam power. He was followed by his brother-in-law Benjamin Frost. The mill was last worked in 1942 and was pulled down in 1954. The mill looks as though it was built at two separate dates if the roof lines are anything to go by.

64. Heybridge was en fete in the 1920s with what looks like the Maldon Band leading the procession. In the background right, can be seen the word 'Ltd' on Bentall's house where the apprentices boarded. Next to it is the Half Moon selling 'Shrimp Brand Beers'. In the centre is the Anchor advertising 'Luncheons and Teas' and left is Mr. Jack Hunter's little wooden building advertising the fact that he was a 'Cycle Engineer, Repairs a Speciality'. In the late 1920s he built a new garage on this site and c1929 he employed a qualified mechanic, Mr. Frederick Came, and entered the motor trade. His garage thus became a service station selling oil and petrol. On either side of the road is a stone wall: the remains of the mediaeval bridge that crossed the River Blackwater at this point. This bridge was rebuilt in 1870 replacing the five arches with two.

MALDON. - HOLLOWAY ROAD, HEYBRIDGE. No.20.

65. Much of pre-eighteenth century Heybridge developed around The Square and westwards along Holloway Road. It was not until the coming of the Navigation after 1797 that the centre of gravity of Heybridge changed so that development took place around the church and the hall. Holloway Road was so called because Jeremiah Holloway was not only living in this road but was one of the principal landowners in Heybridge in 1815. The cottages on the extreme left were owned by Isaac Belsham and those brick and weather boarded cottages on the right were owned by Daniel Belsham in the mid-nineteenth century. Indeed, until well into the twentieth century Isaac Belsham and Son, maltsters, coal and oil cake merchants, had wharfs both sides of the road on the Heybridge side of Black Bridge, from where this photograph was taken c1910. The next row of cottages, left, were owned by Jeremiah Holloway and he lived in a house opposite in c1847. Holloway Road developed enormously at the turn of the century.

66. Heybridge Street c1900. Before c1830 there was not a single building on the right hand side of this road. This strip of land alongside Heybridge Creek was all common land. As Heybridge developed so these narrow sites were built on. In the foreground, right, can be seen the premises of the business which in 1894 was operated by George Fuller. He was an agent, as the notice on the wall proclaims, for Daniell and Sons', ale, stout, porter and spirit. Further along was the Post Office. The second half of this row of cottages belonged in 1847 to Walter Waring and part was occupied by Stephen Bickmore, carpenter. Further along, right, are the 'St Andrew's In Memoriam Schools', built in 1869 by Walter Waring, JP, in memory of his father, a former vicar of Heybridge. The schools closed in 1900. The shop, left, was kept by Arthur Harris, hay and straw dealer. The Heybridge Iron Works, founded in 1816, can be seen in the background. This part of the Works was built in the 1860s and demolished in 1975.

67. In c1894 Fitch wrote that 'we find the quaint little vicarage with its bright garden'. Indeed, from this photograph it looks as though Heybridge Vicarage was at least seventeenth century in date but it was pulled down and replaced by a brick structure in 1908. The living of Heybridge was in the patronage of the Dean and Chapter of St. Paul's and they supported a vicar here. This was the home of Reverend John Pridden MA, FSA, vicar from 1783 to 1797 and local antiquarian, and of Reverend Frances Waring who died in 1833 aged 62 years leaving a widow and nine children. He was vicar for 36 years and master of Maldon Grammar School from 1810 to 1832. He was not the only vicar with a record of longevity, for Reverend Thomas Wren, MA, was here from 1857 to 1894. Reverend T.H. Clark, MA, was vicar here at the turn of the century. To the right can be seen the Norman church and in the background part of Heybridge Iron Works which surrounded the church property on three sides.

Heybridge Street and Hall Road.

68. Although this is commonly called 'The Street', at the turn of the century this was known as 'Church Street'. This view was taken c1905. The properties on the right were built from 1830 onwards and the tall building and the pair of cottages this side of it from c1850. In 1906 the tall building was a shop kept by John Payne and it much later became the Post Office. The Queen's Head, perhaps an indication that it was built at the beginning of Victoria's reign, had a number of landlords. In 1882 James Witney was landlord and he was also a lime burner. Among others he was followed by John Butcher, Frederick Ford and Robert Filbey. Hall Road goes off to the right. The row of houses on the left of Hall Road was built by Bentalls in c1860 on land that had formerly belonged to George Coates, merchant of Springfield. The shop on the corner, extreme left, was owned by the Maldon and Heybridge Co-operative Society.

Canal from Wave Bridge, Heybridge.

69. This view of c1910 shows the two cottages hard by the towing path of the Navigation at Heybridge just north of Wave Bridge. The cottages were probably built soon after the opening of the Navigation in 1797. These two tenements were owned in 1815 by John Russell and in 1847 by William Russell, but were occupied by Charles Rayland and James Frost. On the left can be seen part of Bentall's Iron Works with some barges drawn up at the wharf. The barges brought up coal, timber and lime from Heybridge Basin. When this photograph was taken the towing paths were well used by horses hauling barges to Chelmsford.

Wave Bridge & Canal, Heybridge.

A.H.Judd & Co
Southend.

70. In the background of this view of c1910 can be seen, right, the enormous store that was erected in 1863 by Edward Hammond Bentall (1814-1898), the owner of Heybridge Iron Works. It dominates the Heybridge skyline and was built to store agricultural machinery at a time that Bentall's overseas trade was expanding. When required the machinery was loaded on to barges and taken to the Basin to be put aboard ships destined for all parts of the world. Wave Bridge had to be rebuilt because it had become unsafe. The work was undertaken by the Essex County Council and cost £1,624 and the new bridge was opened on 1 September 1910, by Mr. Vero W. Taylor, CA, Chairman of the County Highways. The building beside the Navigation, right, belonged to George Coates, merchant of Springfield and from c1860 to c1874 this wharf was occupied by Joseph Going, coal, corn, oilcake, guano and salt merchant, who owned canal barges and ships.

Canal at Heybridge.

71. The canal, or strictly speaking, the Navigation, at this point is a completely artificial cut that links Heybridge Basin with Heybridge and was built across Heybridge Marsh. The premises, left, called Navigation Place, built c1800, once formed the Heybridge Brewery, but by 1837 the then owner, Mr. Wells, was selling this freehold estate of ten tenements, with an annual rental of £50 14s, which could be adapted for a malting or a granary. In 1847 Navigation Place was owned by Henry Harridance and William Wright. On the extreme right is a cottage that was built on property owned by Edward Eavery in 1847 but now pulled down. The unladen barge, centre, is being hauled to Heybridge Basin. These barges that plied on the Chelmer and Blackwater were 60 feet long and 16 feet of beam and had a draught of 2 feet. Note the well trimmed towing path of the Navigation in this view of c1905.

THE DRIVE TO "THE TOWERS". 13.

72. Edward Hammond Bentall (1814-1898), son of William Bentall, founder of Heybridge Iron Works, built himself a completely new house in Heybridge in 1873 called The Towers. It was designed by Charles Pertwee, architect, of Chelmsford, but incorporated many of Mr. Bentall's own ideas such as heating by hot air ducts. The house, in the Italianate style, was built with large concrete blocks, and was supposed to have been the first concrete house in Europe. It cost £65,000. A lake was formed to add grandeur to the setting. This view shows the main drive running east-west with the house on the right. Mr. Bentall was Liberal M.P. for Maldon from 1868 to 1874; he was a Nonconformist with many interests in subjects such as astronomy, the protection of certain types of birds, archaeology and yachting, having designed the yacht 'Jullanar'. The Towers was demolished in the 1950s.

Maldon, Heybridge Basin.

73. Originally there was no road access to Heybridge Basin. Only in 1811 with the Heybridge Enclosure Act was such a road link made with Goldhanger Road, but from 1823 to 1836 Borough Marsh Road (now Basin Road) was illegally made a toll road with a gate and toll house at the Goldhanger Road end. In 1836, however with two JPs present (C. Comyms Parker, Esq. and Reverend C. Matthew) to prevent any disturbance, 'the bars of the gate were sawn assunder which released the lock and the gate was thrown open; a cart then proceeded to the Chelmer Basin and returned without payment of toll'. This is a view of Basin Road, taken c1914, just as you leave the Basin. On the right and left can be seen some of the development that had taken place between c1850 and 1875 before the serious economic depression of the mid-1880s.

THE STORES & POST OFFICE, HEYBRIDGE BASIN.

74. Samuel Purkiss set up business at Heybridge Basin c1900 and is first described as a 'shopkeeper' and by 1912 as a 'grocer' and keeper of the Post Office. Together with his son Clifford, Samuel soon had mobile shops and he was probably the first tally man in the area that would allow people goods on credit. Here the horse covered waggon is advertising 'Purkiss and Sons, Drapers and Boot Factors' as well as 'Hosiery'. He had extensive rounds to the north of Heybridge and if his customers from the Totham area required a special order Mr. Purkiss had it sent to the Crown where it could be collected. This view taken in the 1920s shows Samuel and Clifford at the door of their shop, and one horse-drawn and one motorised vehicle outside. In 1928 when the tide washed over the sea wall it was right up to Mr. Purkiss's shop door.

Heybridge Basin.

75. Heybridge Basin was dug out of Heybridge Marsh in 1793 and soon after that date houses were erected to the north of the Basin. The weather boarded cottages were built about 1793 and the building, right, rebuilt in 1858, was the site of the Chelmer Brig Inn that was opened by 1799. During the depression of the 1880s several landlords were unable to make a living here and the license was finally sold for £200 in 1894. In 1902 this house, then called Lock House, was leased to Mr. R.T. Smith, founder of the Homes for Motherless Children and, finally, in 1906 with the popularity of the Basin as a boating, fishing and beauty spot the former Chelmer Brig was opened up as the Old Ship. To the left of the cottages is the granary, now demolished, which was owned by the Navigation Company, and used as a store for perishable cargoes.

76. Mill Beach, c1903, so called because a windmill stood here on the beach until c1892. The Mill House is the white house on the right. In the 1890s Mill Beach became a favourite watering place and by c1900 James Loveday was advertising the Mill Beach Hotel, extreme right, with 'good boating, fishing and bathing'. By 1906 this hotel had been taken over by Benjamin Handley who remained here until the late twenties. By the early 1900s Charles Williams of Heybridge was operating 'conveyances' from Maldon East Station to Mill Beach. In the background is Saltcote where George and Frederick May carried on a malting business and were agents for Watney, Combe, Reid and Co's cask and bottled ales. The 'S.BELLE' indicates that the barge, 'Saltcote Belle', made its way up to Saltcote Wharf. The barge, left, is being loaded up, 'stackie' fashion, with hay to feed the teeming thousands of London's horses.